Contents

Any words appearing in the text in bold, **like this**, are explained in the glossary.

Looking at the weather

What is the weather?

People often talk about the **weather**. This is because it affects so many things we do. The food we eat depends on the weather. Many of the sports we play depend on the weather. Even what we wear changes as the weather changes.

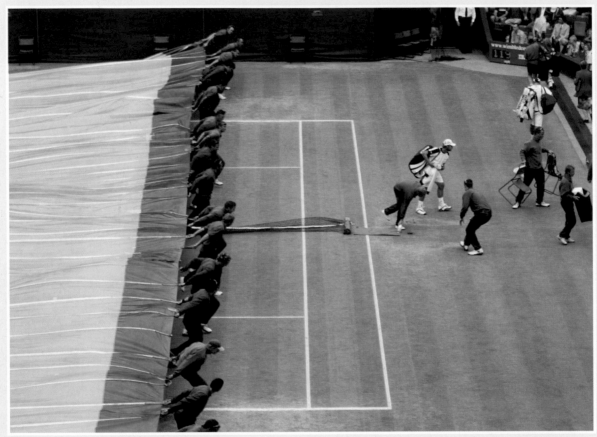

■ *Rain stops play! The ground staff at the Wimbledon tennis championships must be prepared to cover the tennis courts quickly if it rains. Rain makes the grass courts too slippery to play on.*

Always changing

The weather can change every day, and sometimes changes many times in one day. Clear and sunny skies in the morning can change to rain in the afternoon. In the UK, a spell of settled weather is less common than changeable weather.

What makes weather?

The **atmosphere** is the name for the layer of gases that surrounds our planet Earth. As the atmosphere changes, so we get different types of weather. The **temperature** is how hot or cold it is. This is easy for us to feel and to measure. The instrument used to measure temperature is called a **thermometer**.

There is always **water vapour** in the air. Clouds are droplets of cooled water vapour that have collected together. They are a sign that there is lots of water in the air. That water may come down as rain or snow, or stay in the air as **humidity**.

The wind is air moving from one place to another. It can bring warm or cold air. It can also blow clouds of water from the oceans that then fall as rain over the land.

The weather machine

The weather is like a giant machine made from many different parts. A change to one part affects all the other parts. Cooling changes water vapour into clouds. Clouds block out the Sun and make the temperature colder. Differences in heat between places also make the winds blow. No wonder weather forecasters find it so hard to get their predictions right all the time!

■ On hot days people love to eat ice cream.

See for yourself

Go outside or look through your classroom window.

1 What can you see in the sky?
2 Write a description of everything you can see there.
3 Draw a picture of your sky. Can you draw the wind? Have a go.

How do we know what the weather will be like?

The job of studying the **weather** is done by **meteorologists**. They have to understand how the weather works so that they can forecast what will happen next. To do this, they need information about the **temperature**, **humidity**, wind speed, **air pressure,** and other weather features. This information is called **data**.

Getting data

Weather data is recorded by **weather stations** on land and at sea. Weather balloons carrying instruments are sent up in the air. Aircraft also give reports about the weather. **Weather satellites** in space can see the weather all over the world. They measure the temperature of the air and sea. They also show the positions of clouds.

■ *A satellite image is a photograph taken from a satellite in space. In this image you can see storm clouds approaching Florida in the USA.*

Weather patterns

We use satellite images of Earth taken from space to find patterns in the weather. Clouds show that a storm is coming. No clouds show that it is hot and dry. Meteorologists use these patterns to work out what will happen to the weather. We can find weather forecasts on television, on the radio, and in newspapers.

Weather maps

Data about the weather is fed into computers to make weather maps. These help the meteorologists to forecast the weather. Most weather forecasts are accurate for a few days in advance, though sometimes there are mistakes.

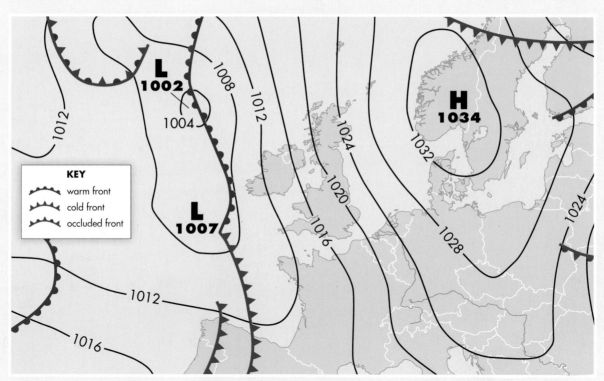

KEY
warm front
cold front
occluded front

■ *Maps like this one help meteorologists predict the weather.*

Using the data

Weather forecasts are needed by many different people. Farmers need to know when it will be best to harvest their crops. Roads need to be gritted or covered with salt when icy weather is expected. People in ships need to know what kind of weather to expect. Sailors have their own shipping forecast because of their special safety needs. This forecast divides the sea into different shipping areas. The waters around the UK are divided into zones with names such as Thames, Lundy, and Dogger.

How can we measure the weather at school?

See for yourself

You are going to see what the **weather** is like in your area for one week. In order to do this, you will need to set up your own **weather station** at school to measure the rainfall and the **temperature**. The instructions are given below.

Measuring rainfall

To make a **rain gauge** you will need: a plastic bottle, a 15-centimetre ruler, and some sticky tape.

1 Mark a line all around the bottle, 10 centimetres from the top.

2 Cut the bottle in two along the line. Take care when using the scissors.

3 Turn the top section upside down and put it into the bottom section. This will make a funnel for the rain.

4 Tape the funnel in place.

5 On a piece of paper make a scale from 0 to 7 centimetres. Mark every 5 millimetres.

6 Tape this scale to the outside of the bottle, making sure zero is at the bottom.

7 Take your rain gauge outside to a secure site where it will not fall over.

8 At the same time each day, read the scale to find out how much rain is in the gauge. Make sure your readings are accurate. Remember to empty the gauge afterwards.

■ *A rain gauge measures the amount of rainfall over a given period of time.*

Measuring temperature

Hang a large **thermometer** from a tree branch to measure the air temperature. Make at least three readings a day, so you can compare temperatures over the day.

Results

Set your weather station equipment up in the playground and record your findings in a chart like this:

	Rain (mm)	Temperature (°C)
Monday		
Tuesday		
Wednesday		
Thursday		
Friday		

Make up three of these tables: one for 9:00 a.m. the second for 12:00 p.m. and the third for 3:00 p.m. You can then see how the weather changes during the day.

■ A thermometer measures how hot or cold the air is. In the Celsius scale, water freezes at 0 °C and boils at 100 °C.

Exploring further

You might also like to measure the wind at school. Go to the Heinemann Explore website or CD-ROM and click on Exploring > Weather outside your school. Read the article 'Measuring the weather at school' to learn how to do it.

Different kinds of weather

Sunny weather

People in the UK and in many other countries usually look forward to sunny days. Farmers know that their crops need sunlight in order to grow. Many activities, such as sporting events, need dry, sunny **weather** to be really fun. We value sunny days because our weather is often unsettled for long periods.

■ *Plants need sunlight as well as water and nutrients to grow well.*

Activity

We can only do certain activities when the weather is sunny. In a table like the one below, list all the things you can think of that need sunny weather. In the second column, draw a picture to illustrate the activity.

Activity	Drawing

Frequent sunshine

In some countries, such as Egypt and Australia, it is sunny for days or even months at a time. In places like this, people often hope or pray for rain. They need it to make the crops grow, and often enjoy it as a change from the heat.

Up in the air

We have sunny weather when there are few or no clouds in the sky. Clouds only form when warm, wet air rises and cools. The moisture in the air cools to form clouds.

- *In the Sahara **Desert** there is very little water in the air. This means there are very few clouds and very little rain. It is sunny for about 361 days of the year.*

Why are clear skies blue?

Sunlight looks white, but it is really a mixture of all the colours of the rainbow. When light from the Sun passes through the **atmosphere** it hits **water vapour** and tiny bits of dust in the air. The light is scattered in all directions. Blue is scattered more than the other colours, so we see more of it. This is why the sky looks blue.

Exploring further

Go to the Heinemann Explore website or CD-ROM. Click on Resources > Weather outside your window. Look at the map showing the average hours of sunshine per day in the UK. Which areas are the most sunny? Which areas are the least sunny? Now look in Digging Deeper > Sunshine and clouds. Find out how the Sun affects the temperature by reading the article 'The Sun and temperature'.

Rain and snow

Water that falls from the clouds is called **precipitation**. Precipitation can fall as rain, drizzle, hail, snow, or sleet.

Rain factories

We can describe clouds as rain factories. These factories need water to help them make rain. Air contains water in the form of **water vapour**. If the water vapour cools, it turns into tiny drops of liquid water and forms clouds.

Some clouds form high in the sky where the air **temperature** is below freezing. It may be so cold that the water droplets freeze into tiny ice crystals. These join up to form snowflakes, which then drift down through the cloud. As they move into warmer air they melt and make raindrops. These drops fall to the ground as rain.

■ *A snowflake is made up of ice crystals.*

Sleet and snow

In winter, the air below the cloud is also cold. This allows the snowflakes to fall to Earth without melting. The snow that falls in very cold weather feels dry and powdery. This is because the snowflakes have not melted at all. Sometimes the snowflakes melt a little as they fall. This 'wet' snow is good for making snowmen because it sticks together well. Sleet is very wet snow.

Hail

Sometimes the winds inside the clouds swirl around. The winds pick up falling raindrops and take them up into the colder air again. The raindrops join with other droplets and freeze. They start to fall, but are thrown upwards again. This time the frozen drops get even bigger and form ice balls. Eventually, these ice balls fall from the clouds as hailstones.

■ *Travelling by car in a hailstorm can be a frightening experience. It is hard to see where you are going and the road quickly becomes slippery.*

Drizzle

If the clouds are very low in the sky, the tiny droplets of water form so near the ground that they fall before they have joined together to make raindrops. Instead, they fall as drizzle or form mist and fog.

Exploring further

Go to the Heinemann Explore website or CD-ROM. Click on Resources > Weather outside your window. Look at the animation showing drizzle, rain, sleet, and snow. In Resources > Wild weather look at the video of a blizzard. Think about what it would feel like to be out in this kind of weather.

Windy weather

The movement of air above and around us is called wind. Wind is caused by changes in **air pressure**. Air pressure is how hard the air is pressing against the Earth's surface. When air is warmed, it becomes lighter and presses down less. When air cools, it becomes heavier and presses down more. This means that warm air has low pressure and cold air has higher pressure.

■ *As air is warmed, it loses pressure and rises. Cooler, high-pressure air rushes in underneath it. This causes a wind. Getting out and about in a strong wind can be difficult!*

In the UK, the wind most often comes from the south-west. This wind helps create weather that is mostly wet and mild. The coldest days in the UK are during the winter, when the wind blows from the north or the east.

The Beaufort scale

We measure how fast a wind is blowing using the Beaufort scale. The scale starts at 0, when there is no wind, and goes up to force 12, which is a **hurricane**. A hurricane has a wind speed of more than 118 kilometres (73 miles) per hour.

Force	The wind's strength and what happens
1	Smoke drifts slowly. Leaves on trees hardly move at all.
2	Drifting smoke clearly shows the direction the wind is going.
3	Gentle winds. Leaves rustle and you can feel the wind on your face.
4	Moderate winds. Leaves are constantly moving. Dust blows around.
5	Small trees sway and paper blows away.
6	Strong winds. Large branches of trees sway.
7	Winds are stronger still. Whole trees sway.
8	Gales. Tree twigs break. It is hard to walk.
9	Branches of trees break. Roof tiles are blown down.
10	Small trees are uprooted. Roofs are damaged.
11	Violent storms. Buildings are damaged. Larger trees are uprooted. It is not possible to walk.
12	Hurricane winds. Much is destroyed. Anything unsecured is lifted off the ground.

Activity

Using the information in the table above, make a colourful poster to help people understand the wind forces shown by the Beaufort scale.

■ The winds associated with hurricanes can cause a huge amount of damage.

Weather around the world

In geography it is important to know about and understand the different **climates** in the world. An area's climate includes the **temperatures** and the amount of rainfall it usually has. The climate affects what goes on in an area.

How do you find the hot places in the world?

You can look at a map of the world and use the **latitude** lines to find the hot places. Lines of latitude are imaginary lines that go horizontally (sideways) around the Earth. The most important line of latitude is the **equator**. This is an imaginary line around the middle of the Earth. The areas to the north and south of the equator are the hottest on Earth.

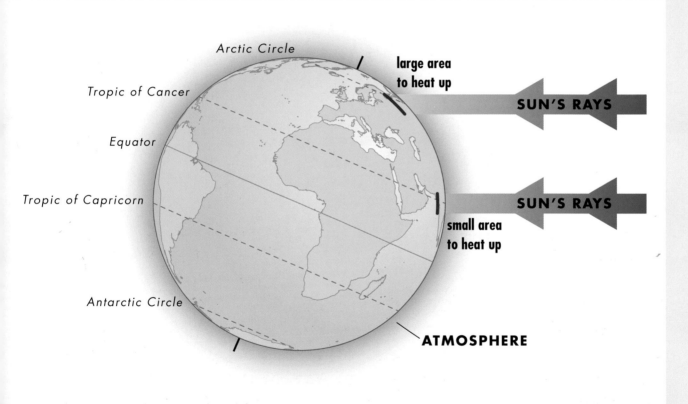

■ At the equator the Sun shines over the Earth at a steep angle, which means it is almost directly overhead. When the heat from the Sun is spread over a small area its heating power is strong, so the area feels very hot.

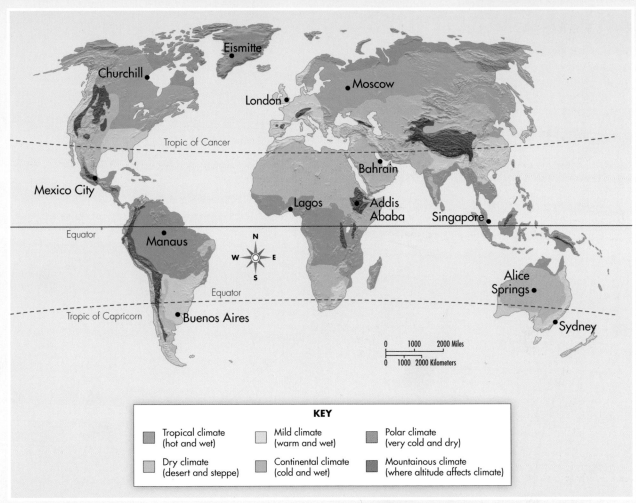

Churchill
Eismitte
Moscow
London
Tropic of Cancer
Bahrain
Mexico City
Lagos
Addis Ababa
Singapore
Equator
Manaus
Alice Springs
Equator
Tropic of Capricorn
Buenos Aires
Sydney

0   1000   2000 Miles
0   1000   2000 Kilometers

KEY

Tropical climate
(hot and wet)

Mild climate
(warm and wet)

Polar climate
(very cold and dry)

Dry climate
(desert and steppe)

Continental climate
(cold and wet)

Mountainous climate
(where altitude affects climate)

■ *The hottest places on Earth are between the equator and the **Tropic of Cancer** and the **Tropic of Capricorn**. The coldest places on Earth are found at the **North Pole** and the **South Pole**.*

How do you find cold places in the world?

The coldest places on Earth are at its most northern and southern points. The Sun never shines high above these areas, so the land does not get very warm. You can use the latitude lines on your map to find these areas too. In the **northern hemisphere**, the coldest region lies to the north of the **Arctic Circle**. In the **southern hemisphere,** the coldest region lies to the south of the **Antarctic Circle**.

Exploring further

On the Heinemann Explore website or CD-ROM find out more about the weather near the equator. Go to Exploring > Weather around the world and read the article 'Tropical weather'. You could also try out the activity related to this article.

How does the weather affect human activity?

Many things that we do are affected by the **weather**. The weather can make it unsafe to do an activity or spoil our enjoyment of it.

Hot weather

Many things we do are more enjoyable in warm, sunny weather, such as swimming outside, having a picnic, or playing in the park. Other activities are much harder to do when it is hot. It may not be possible to do energetic activities, such as running, if it is too hot. They will make you very hot and tired and also possibly **dehydrated**. It can be tiring just walking about in really hot weather!

Activity

Think of all the outdoor activities you enjoy. List the ones that can be done in each of these types of weather:

1 hot weather
2 rainy weather
3 cool weather
4 snowy weather.

■ *A cricket match needs dry weather, and can be very pleasant to play in or watch on a warm, sunny day.*

Cold weather

We can only do activities like skiing and sledging in really cold weather when there is snow on the ground. However, if the weather is bitterly cold you need to wear suitable clothing or you could become too cold.

Cloudy or misty weather

Misty or cloudy weather can make it difficult to see properly. This can make journeys by car, plane, or boat more dangerous, or even impossible.

Rainy weather

Light rain will not harm you, but if you get very wet you may feel cold and uncomfortable. This might stop you from going outside on a wet day.

In very wet weather flooding can occur. Flood water can cause serious problems. During a major flood, water and mud can destroy homes and other buildings, and drown plants, animals, and people.

■ *This flood in Carlisle in January 2005 caused a huge amount of damage to people's houses. This woman is being rescued from her flooded home.*

How does the weather affect where we go on holiday?

Why do people go on holiday?

We enjoy going on holiday. It gives us a break from going to work or school. There are many different types of holiday, for example a beach holiday, a visit to a theme park, or camping. The **weather** is usually an important factor when we choose a holiday. We want it to be hot and dry if we are going on a beach holiday, and snow is very important if we want to go skiing or sledging.

■ *Many people choose to go on holiday to places such as Egypt, where they know it will be hot and sunny.*

Activity

1 When you go on holiday, where do you like to go? Is the weather important to your choice? Think about the types of activities you like to do on holiday, and how the weather influences them.

2 Ask some of your friends about their holidays. Make up a chart like the one below.

Name	Where would you most like to go on holiday?	What is the weather like there?

Activity

1 Think about the last holiday you went on. Where did you go? What did you do?

2 Describe your holiday to a friend. You will need to tell them about these points:

   • Where the place is. Which country it is in.

   • Whether it is in a hot or cold part of the world, and what the weather is like there.

   • What it is actually like. You could describe the town or village, the buildings, houses, shops, tourist places, and beaches, for example.

   • Any famous sites that are nearby.

   • The kinds of activities you can do there.

Exploring further

Look at the articles listed below on the Heinemann Explore website or CD-ROM to find out more about the weather in different parts of the world. Look under Exploring > Weather around the world. Think about how the weather in each region will affect whether people go there for holidays or not:

• **desert** weather

• **tropical** weather

• **temperate** weather

• weather in the **polar** regions.

Where can we go on holiday?

Every year many people ask themselves this question. They will want to use their break as a time to relax or to do an activity that interests them.

What can I do?

There are so many places you can visit on holiday. Your choice of place depends on what you want to do when you get there. If you were planning a trip for someone who was interested in wild animals, you might suggest they go on **safari**, maybe to a **National Park** in Africa.

If the person liked relaxing in the sun and swimming, you might suggest a beach holiday somewhere warm where they could swim in the sea, such as on the coast of the Mediterranean Sea in Spain, Greece, or Italy.

Activity

1 Make a list of the kinds of weather that are best for these activities:
   * football and rugby
   * outdoor swimming and **scuba diving**
   * skiing
   * hill walking.

2 Think of suitable places in the world where people can do each of these activities.

■ *Countries like Kenya and Botswana in Africa are ideal holiday destinations for people who like to get close to wildlife.*

A holiday to somewhere snowy is ideal for people who enjoy winter sports. A ski resort, such as Val d'Isère in France or Whistler in Canada, would suit them. They would need to be prepared for the cold weather, especially in Canada where temperatures can fall to –30 °C.

An interesting holiday for a walker is to travel to Peru, in South America, and follow the trail of the **Incas**. The weather in this region is usually dry and sunny, but it can be unpredictable as it is in the mountains.

■ *Walkers on the Inca Trail in Peru hope for dry, sunny weather on their route.*

What do we need to take with us?

You need to ask yourself this question when you are getting ready to go on holiday. The answer will depend a lot on the **weather**. If you went skiing and only packed shorts and T-shirts you would freeze!

■ *A snowboarder in the cold mountains needs to wear very warm clothes.*

■ *A sunhat is essential in countries where the weather is hot and sunny all day.*

Activity

1 Write lists of the clothes you would need to pack for the following types of holiday. Look on the Internet to see what the weather will be like in each place at the time of year given:

- snowboarding in Canada during January
- walking in Peru during June
- sightseeing in Jordan during August.

2 Imagine you are on the snowboarding trip in Canada during January. Write a postcard home describing how the weather has affected what you have done so far.

Clothes for different destinations

For a variety of countries around the world we can look at their typical weather and decide which clothes are most suitable for a summer holiday in each place.

Country	Continent	Climate	Clothes
Fiji	Oceania	**Tropical**, wet season from November to April.	T-shirts, shorts, light raincoat. Lightweight clothes. Sun cream and sun hats.
Iran	Asia	Cold winters, hot summers. Dry all the time.	Women and girls should be covered in public – it is the law in Iran.
Finland	Europe	Mainly cold **temperate**, so cool summers.	Lightweight jumpers, trousers. Warm coats for the evening.
Congo	Central Africa	Tropical – rainy season March to June, dry season June to October.	Plenty of changes of T-shirts and shorts, and an umbrella.
Sudan	Africa	Hot and mainly dry	Lots of sun cream and a hat, lightweight clothes that cover the arms to prevent burning.
Canada	North America	Cool temperate, so cool summers, cold winters and fairly wet.	Light jumpers and trousers for the day and warm clothes for the evening.
Venezuela	South America	Tropical – wet season May to November.	Lots of changes of lightweight clothes.
Greenland	North America	**Polar**	Very warm clothing including thermal underwear, gloves, scarves, and warm hats that cover your ears.

How are places similar to and different from our own locality?

In geography it is important to know and understand about different places in the world. We can do this by comparing them with where we live.

See for yourself

Go for a walk around the area where you live. Read about the places described below. How are they similar to or different from your own area? Think about these questions:

- Where is it?
- What is the **weather** like?
- What is the landscape like?
- Are there any special features?

Barcelona, Spain

Barcelona is a city on the north-east coast of Spain, in a region called Cataluña. The weather is hot in summer and cool in winter. It can have a lot of rain in winter. Barcelona is surrounded by hilly land and is not far from a mountain called Montserrat. It is also near the coast. There are many interesting features, including the streets called the Ramblas, the church of the Holy Family designed by a 20th-century architect called Gaudì, and a replica of Christopher Columbus's ship the *Santa Maria*.

■ *In Barcelona the Ramblas are tree-lined promenades leading from the Plaza de Cataluña, which is the largest square in Spain.*

Patagonia, Argentina

Patagonia is on the southern tip of South America. The weather is cool in summer and cold in winter. The landscape is mountainous, and includes part of the Andes mountain range. There are many **glaciers** and lakes.

■ *This is the Perito Moreno Glacier in Patagonia.*

Wellington, New Zealand

Wellington is a city on the southern tip of New Zealand's North Island. It has hot summers and cool winters, and a reasonable amount of rain. The city is surrounded by lots of inlets and forested hills. Its special features include a large museum called Te Papa, beautiful **botanical gardens**, and a cable car.

■ *Wellington is surrounded by lush green hills that are covered in forests.*

Which places have you visited?

Make a factfile like the ones opposite for the countries you have visited or would like to visit. Include the following information:

- the name of the country

- the name of the **continent** the country is in

- what the **weather** is like there

- what **climate** zone the country is in

- how many people live there

- what languages they speak.

You could add more information to your factfile, and even include photographs.

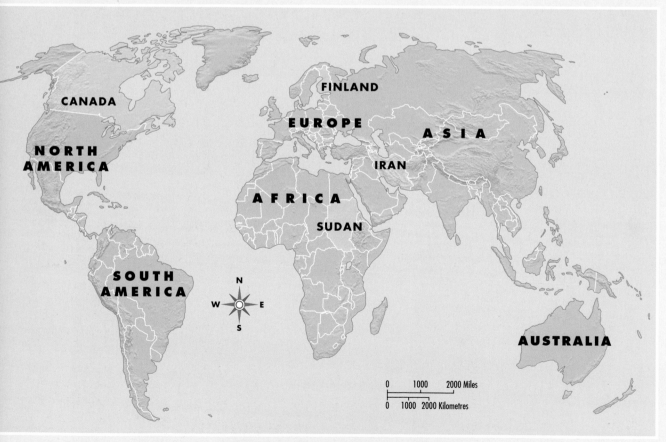

■ *This map shows the locations of Iran, Finland, Sudan, and Canada.*

Iran

- Official name: Islamic Republic of Iran
- Capital city: Tehran
- Population: 70.3 million
- Continent: Asia
- Weather: hot and dry
- Climatic zone: **desert**
- Official language: Farsi (Persian)

Finland

- Official name: Republic of Finland
- Capital city: Helsinki
- Population: 5.1 million
- Continent: Europe
- Weather: cool in summer, cold in winter
- Climatic zone: cold **temperate**, **polar** inside the **Arctic Circle**
- Official languages: Finnish, Swedish

Sudan

- Official name: Republic of the Sudan
- Capital city: Khartoum
- Population: 34.5 million
- Continent: Africa
- Weather: hot and dry
- Climatic zone: desert
- Official language: Arabic

Canada

- Official name: Canada
- Capital city: Ottawa
- Population: 31 million
- Continent: North America
- Weather: cool in summer, cold in winter
- Climatic zone: cool temperate, polar inside the Arctic Circle
- Official languages: English, French

Glossary

air pressure how hard the air is pressing against the Earth's surface

Antarctic Circle cold area around the South Pole

Arctic Circle cold area around the North Pole

atmosphere layer of gases that surrounds the Earth

Beaufort scale system of recording how fast the wind is blowing

botanical gardens place where special plants are kept and studied

climate average weather conditions over a long period of time

continent huge mass of land that may have many different countries on it. Europe is a continent, so is Africa.

data detailed measurements and information, for example about elements of the weather

dehydrated when your body does not have enough water

desert large area of very dry, often sandy land

equator imaginary line around the middle of the Earth

glacier slow moving river of ice

humidity amount of water in the air

hurricane very strong wind, with a speed of more than 118 kilometres (73 miles) per hour

Incas South American Indian people who lived in the Andes before the mid 1500s

latitude distance north or south from the Equator

meteorologist person who studies the weather

National Park area of landscape that is protected because of its natural beauty

northern hemisphere northern half of the Earth, above the equator

North Pole most northerly point on Earth

polar to do with the North or South Pole

precipitation water that falls from the clouds, such as rain, drizzle, hail, snow, or sleet

rain gauge instrument for measuring the amount of rain that falls

safari journey, especially to see wild animals

scuba diving diving underwater with a tank of air to breathe from

southern hemisphere southern half of the globe, below the equator

South Pole most southerly point on Earth

temperate where the temperatures are not extreme and rainfall is steady throughout the year

temperature how hot or cold a substance is

thermometer instrument used to measure temperature

Tropic of Cancer latitude line around the Earth at about 23° north of the equator

Tropic of Capricorn latitude line around the Earth at about 23° south of the equator

tropical regions of the world near the equator where it is hot and humid all year round

weather the condition of the atmosphere at one point in time, which can change every day

weather satellite satellite in space that collects data about the weather

weather station place where weather data is recorded

water vapour water as a gas

Find out more

Books

Measuring the weather: Temperature; Rain and snow; Sunshine and clouds; Forecasting the weather; Wind and air pressure, Alan Rodgers and Angella Strelluk (Heinemann Library, 2002)

Wild weather: Big freeze; Blizzard; Drought; Thunderstorm; Heatwave; Tornado; Hurricane, Catherine Chambers (Heinemann Library, 2003)

Websites

www.met-office.gov.uk
Find out all about weather forecasting in the UK. See the weather forecast for the world, and discover more about different types of weather.

www.heinemannexplore.com
Check out the weather section of the Heinemann Explore website to learn more about the weather. You can see videos and animation and try out some activities.

Index

Investigating
the weather

Caroline Clissold

Heinemann

www.heinemann.co.uk/library

Visit our website to find out more information about **Heinemann Library** books.

To order:

☎ Phone 44 (0) 1865 888066

📄 Send a fax to 44 (0) 1865 314091

💻 Visit the Heinemann Bookshop at www.heinemann.co.uk/library to browse our catalogue and order online.

First published in Great Britain by Heinemann Library, Halley Court, Jordan Hill, Oxford OX2 8EJ, part of Harcourt Education. Heinemann is a registered trademark of Harcourt Education Ltd.

Editorial: Vicki Yates
Design: Dave Poole and Tokay Interactive Limited (www.tokay.co.uk)
Illustrations: Geoff Ward and International Mapping (www.internationalmapping.com)
Picture Research: Hannah Taylor
Production: Duncan Gilbert

Originated by Repro Multi Warna
Printed in China by WKT Company Limited

10 digit ISBN: 0 431 03256 4   (Hardback)
13 digit ISBN: 978 0 431 03256 6 (Hardback)
10 09 08 07 06
10 9 8 7 6 5 4 3 2 1

10 digit ISBN: 0 431 03263 7   (Paperback)
13 digit ISBN: 978 0 431 03263 4 (Paperback)
10 09 08 07 06
10 9 8 7 6 5 4 3 2 1

British Library Cataloguing in Publication Data
Clissold, Caroline
Investigating the weather
551.6
A full catalogue record for this book is available from the British Library.

Acknowledgements
Alamy Images p. **10** (James Osmond), p. **20** (Nicholas Pitt), p. **24l** (Thinkstock), p. **24r** (Tribaleye Images); Comstock Images p. **9**; Corbis Royalty Free p. **5b**, p. **26**, p. **27b**; Corbis p. **4** (Reuters/ Alastair Grant), p. **15** (Dallas Morning News/Irwin Thompson), p. **19** (Reuters/Jeff Mitchell), p. **23** (Reuters/Pilar Olivares), p. **27t** (Steve Kaufman); Getty Images pp. **5t**, **22** (The Image Bank), p. **12** (Taxi), p. **18** (Stone); Harcourt Education Ltd p. **8** (Tudor Photography); Photodisc pp. **6**, **11**; Rex Features p. **14**, p. **13** (Kevin Wheal).

Cover photograph of umbrellas in the rain, reproduced with permission of Getty Images/Digital Vision.

The publishers would like to thank Rebecca Harman, Rachel Bowles, Robyn Hardyman, and Caroline Landon for their assistance in the preparation of this book.

Every effort has been made to contact copyright holders of any material reproduced in this book. Any omissions will be rectified in subsequent printings if notice is given to the publishers.

All the Internet addresses (URLs) given in this book were valid at the time of going to press. However, due to the dynamic nature of the Internet, some addresses may have changed, or sites may have changed or ceased to exist since publication. While the author and Publishers regret any inconvenience this may cause readers, no responsibility for any such changes can be accepted by either the author or the Publishers.

Exploring further

Throughout this book you will find links to the Heinemann Explore CD-ROM and website at www.heinemannexplore.com. Follow the links to find out more about the topic.